In Bloom

For my mother.

Roots 5

Seedling 17

In Bloom 45

Roots

In Bloom

Your eyes are closed.
I lay very still, waiting.

Exhale. Inhale. Exhale.

Some nights I stay awake
counting your breaths

(counting my blessings).

-Mother

From my father's rose garden
I learned of beauty
and of pain.

From my father's rose garden
I learned of caution
and of persistence.

And when the garden withered
I learned grief
and I learned resilience.

-Rose

In Bloom

It is said that heaven lies under your mother's feet.
Let me stay awhile
in the shade of my mother
the same way
I hid in the velvet darkness
of her womb.

I find solace in every part of you.

-Refuge

There are times when I ache
for the comforts of a homeland
I can never call home
and for the beauty of a language
that will never sit easily
on my tongue.

There are times when I mourn
for the land you left behind
for the culture I have half-lost
and for the family that will always
feel like strangers.

How could you bring yourself
to leave yourself behind?

-Emigrating

In Bloom

From my mother
I learned strength
I learned fierceness
I learned resilience.

From my father
I learned softness
I learned ease
I learned laughter.

Tell me again
how strength is found only in men.

-Strength

There was a time

(when I was young and foolish and
full of shame
for the vibrancy
of my culture)

when I longed to hide.

There was a time
I would smother the rich colors of my heritage

saffron
        turmeric
                brown
                        black

in bland shades of white.

(I wanted to be just like them, you see).

No longer.

-Acceptance

You are a warrior.

I know you do not feel like such.
I know you are weary, dear one –
but you are a warrior.
You have fought this life

(with its toil and bleakness and pain)

you have fought this life
and you have won.

Hand me your weapons, dear one –
you have earned this rest
(many times over).

Let me fight for you now.

-Handoff

For every harsh word I have said –
forgive me.
For every tear I called to your eye –
forgive me.
For every moment of worry I caused –
forgive me.
For every instant I forgot that heaven lies beneath your feet –
(your treasured, tired feet)
forgive me.

My mother, my mother, my mother.

-Apology

You have put down roots in this strange land
(you have put down roots in me).

I tether you to this land
just as you tether me
to the land of your mother.

You are the only home I have ever known
and I have rooted myself
in your soil.

This world will always feel strange to me.

And you –
you will always feel like home to me.

-Home

I have caught
a piece of the moon
in my hands.

Somehow
it does not shine
as brightly
up close.

(Perhaps, some things are meant to be admired
only from afar).

-Closeup

In Bloom

She is ruined, they say.
I look
and she is the same to me
as she has always been.
Perhaps
a little worn
perhaps
a heaviness in her step.

(These are the signs of heartache, you see).

There is no sign of ruin.

I wonder
how it is
that the suffering of others
makes monsters of us all.

-Shaming

Seedling

In Bloom

You take my hand
gently
and my heart blooms.

(It is yours).

You let go
and my heart withers.

(But it is still yours).

-Yours

Your hands reach for me
and I recoil.
I have not yet learned
to love myself.
I am not ready
for the love of another.

-Ready

You linger in my mind
the same way
fog lingers
in the early pre-dawn.

(You linger silently
yet
you are everywhere).

If only
my thoughts of you
dissipated
so easily.

-Linger

I would launch
a thousand ships
in your name
if it meant
you would return
to me.

I would cry
a thousand tears
in your wake
if it meant
you would glance back
to me

(just once, darling –

only once).

You are gone
and nothing I do
will entice you
back to me.

-Return

In Bloom

There is a knot in my chest
that twists and aches and throbs
when I look at you.

(I love you the same way I always have).

But something in you
has changed.
Something vital
has shifted with the days.

All I know
is when I look at you
I see
a stranger.

(It hurts to look at you).

-Stranger

The night breathes heavily.
He is gasping
chest heaving
his fingers desperately
seeking
seeking
seeking.

The moon is missing
and the night
aches
the same way I did
when you
walked away from me.

(The moon, at least, is bound to return).

-Unrequited

In Bloom

I am afraid
my heart has
remained
in the cave of solitude
for so long
that it will be blind
to love

(should it shine upon me).

-Blind

And just like that
you became my moon.

(How I wish
I could have been
to you
what you were
to me).

-Wish

In Bloom

How is it
that you give yourself
to me
so easily.

How is it
that your heart
opens
like a flower
blooming
in sunlight.

You have given me
a gift
I do not know how
to accept.

(My heart is locked and I cannot find the key).

-Locked

I used to break myself
into pieces
every night
so you could hold me
in your hands.

It was not until
much later
that I learned
I do not need to limit myself

(I do not need to make myself small)

for you.

-Accommodating

In Bloom

The caravan of our dreams
lay shattered
at my feet.

I gaze at the remnants
of us

(in one piece – feet tangled together in a sunlit bed

        in another – our footsteps in the
        far corners of the world

                in a third – a child with
                your eyes and my mouth)

the kaleidoscope of what
could have been.

I gaze at the remnants
and slowly

(my limbs are heavy with heartbreak)

begin to gather the pieces
of myself.

Recall, darling
what it means to endure.

-Recovery

Sleep beckoned
gently
luring me
with whispers
of you.

I went
knowing that
the bliss
she promised
would be followed
only
by pain.

(Your absence hurts most when I wake from dreams of you).

-Sleep

In Bloom

Love bloomed in my heart
and in my eyes
but my lips remained silent.
You waited
but I could say nothing

and so we parted.

-First Love

So many nights I have spent
watching the moon
haunted
by thoughts of you.

If only you would grant me some respite
and wane with the moon.

-Restless

When we met
I did not know
you would become

the lifeblood of my veins
the sound of my heartbeat
the whisper of my breath.

(Oh, darling
how I wish
I had never met you).

-Regret

Your attempts
to hide your tears
cause me more pain
than I can bear.

Teach me how to soothe you.

-Tears

In Bloom

You touch me gently
as if I am a rare orchid
in bloom
or the morning dewdrop
that trembles
upon the leaf.

You do not know
I am made of stronger stuff than this.

-Composition

You put roots down in my heart.
Our garden was beautiful
but when you left
your roots remained.

-Rooted

In Bloom

There are times when I feel left behind
by this life.
The same way the dandelion remains
after its seeds have dispersed –
gently
gently
life has drifted away from me.

-Dandelion

Your hand in my hand
is a feeling
I will always want
to know.

(I pray you won't let go).

-Hand

In Bloom

Once
I tried to force a feeling
that was not there.
A feeling
that could never be there.

I did not want to be alone.

(But there are worse things, I learned,
than to be alone).

I would rather bloom alone
than wither together.

-Solitude

Some days
I wake
with dreams of you
lingering
in my mind
like morning dew.

These are the mornings
I long for most –
the mornings
where
your path
and mine
are the same

(but no longer).

-Dream

In Bloom

I will never
play the game
in which
whoever
cares less
wins
every time.

I will not
muffle myself
into apathy
just to have
your attention.

My feelings for you are an ocean inside me.

(They will not be contained).

-Game

Too many nights
I have spent
in want of sleep
(in want of you).

No longer.

-Longing

I hold your hand
in my hand
as you sleep.

You breathe
deeply
easily
peacefully.

I trace the lines
of your palm
wondering
if our story
is written there –
wondering
if our love
is meant
to last.

-Palm

My heart has broken
a thousand times
in the wake
of your silence.

I would let it break
a thousand times more
just to hear you say
you love me.

-Break

Who, darling
can we blame
for our own misfortune?

You promised
to meet me in the garden
by moonlight

and I promised
to be there.

Who, darling
can we blame
when both of us lied?

(You did not wait and I never arrived).

-Promise

In Bloom

In Bloom

Speak to me, flower
of what it means
to bloom.

Tell me
what it means
to take root
and bud

what it means
to flourish

(what it means to *endure*).

Speak to me, blossom
of what it means
to bloom.

-Bloom

Your hand is warm in mine.
I raise it to my lips
feel your pulse pounding.

You do not complete me
(for I complete myself)
but with you
I am more.

-More

In Bloom

There is a garden inside of me
where battles have been won and lost
where love has bloomed and withered.

Come, wanderer –
stay awhile.
Plant your seeds.

-Garden

There is
a whole world
out beyond
my reach.

Yet I want you.

(Just you, darling –
only you).

-You

In Bloom

My love is a rare flower.
It blooms only by starlight
and waxes and wanes
with the moon.

Stay, darling
our time is limited.

Let us make the most of it.

-Fleeting

My favorite moments
are the quiet ones
when I can hear
your heart
beating
next to mine.

I wonder –
does your heart
say my name
in every moment
the way mine does
with you?

(My heart beats only for you).

-Name

In Bloom

You take me into your arms
and I curve
into your embrace
(but I do not break).

Darling,
we are a garden of our own.

-Together

There is sweetness on your lips
and poison
on your tongue.

You lure me
with honeyed words
and
promises
full of saccharine deception.

(Darling,
who wounded you so
badly
that you seek only
pain in your pain?)

I willingly follow you
to my own breaking.

(Perhaps, then, I may soothe yours).

-Pain

In Bloom

There are nights
when I sit
and talk with the moon.

Beauty,
you are so far
from the sun –

do you not ever despair?

She lets out a sound
part-sigh
part-moan
and speaks.

There is an odd pleasure
in longing for a love
you know
is already yours.

-Distance

You crept slowly
into my heart.
So slowly
that when finally
I noticed

it was far too late.

My heart
does not know
love
if it does not
know you.

-Love

Do not come to me
seeking peace.

I am a storm
of
uncertainty and anger and despair
beauty and elation and serenity.

Come to me
if you want to live
and live fiercely.

-Human

On the nights
I miss you
I talk to the moon.

She does not remind me
of you
but
she brings me a measure
of the tranquility
I have only ever found
with you.

-Peace

Darling,
if I asked you
(with my hand held out to you)
to walk with me
on a journey
of our own making –
what would you say?

If I asked you
(with my heart held out to you)
to walk with me
on a path
we cannot see –
what would you say?

If I asked you, darling
to be mine –
what would you say?

(I am already yours).

-Marriage

Understand, darling,
that I too
once knew
(so very intimately)
the anxiety
lingering in your eyes.

You cannot let
the fear of wilting
prevent
your bloom.

-Fear

In Bloom

I hold my heart
out to you
and my hands
tremble.

I have given my heart into your keeping
(it is yours now
to do with
as you will).

Be gentle, darling.

-Gift

Lay with me
in the moonlight.

Come morning
we will be new again.

-Renew

In Bloom

I look at you
and my heart feels
so full
(of joy of love of *you*)
it almost hurts.

If I could bottle
this feeling
and keep it forever
I would.

(Would you stay forever, instead?)

-Keep

I am restless tonight.
You notice
and grip my hand tightly
(somehow, my heart aches more at this).

I do not know
how to tell you
that a part of me
longs for the beauty of this world
as strongly
as a part of me
longs for you.

(I crave the open road as much as I crave you).

-Wanderer

In Bloom

Do not ask me
to vocalize
my love for you.

I have not learned
to open myself
in this way

(not yet).

Ask me instead
to show you.

(Oh, darling – I have so much to show you).

-Show

The space
between my heartbeats
is filled
with your name.

I am never without you.

-Heartbeat

In Bloom

Your smile
against my lips
is one of my favorite joys
of this life.

-Joy

You light up
my heart
the same way
the moon
lights
the night sky.

It is no wonder then
that in your absence
I stay with the moon.

-Absence

In Bloom

Recall, darling
the price we paid
for our love.

I will gladly pay it again
if it means
a moment more
with you.

(There is nothing I would not do
to be with you).

-Price

The taste of you
is the sweetest delicacy
I have ever known.

Let me savor you, darling.

-Taste

Come to me
under moonlight
when the world is new again.

Come to me
under starshine
when the world is quiet again.

Come to me
under sunbeams
when the world is bright again.

Come to me
always

(I will always await you).

-Always

S.I. Siddiqui

I see you
behind my eyelids
and in the spaces
between
my fingers.

I see you always, my dear.

(You reside in every part of me).

-Vision

In Bloom

The earth is soft and brown and warm
under the midday sun.
Recall, flower –
this is your home.
(We are all made of the same stuff).

Remember, blossom –
some of us grow
strong and unyielding
others
limber and flexible
others still
gentle and delicate.

Decide, petalled-one –
you write your own destiny.

-Flower

www.ingramcontent.com/pod-product-compliance
Lightning Source LLC
Chambersburg PA
CBHW061341040426
42444CB00011B/3035